Anthony and Elizabeth Duquette Foundation for the Living Arts
presents

OUR LADY
QUEEN OF THE ANGELS
A Celebrational Environment
BY TONY DUQUETTE

With an Original "Saeta" in Verse
BY RAY BRADBURY

Narrated by
Charlton Heston
with music specially composed by
Garth Hudson

Tony Duquette

About the Artist:

Tony Duquette is a world-renowned Los Angeles artist, and the only American to have had a one-man show at the Pavillion de Marsan of the Louvre, Paris. He has created this celebrational environment as a gift for Los Angeles on its 200th birthday. His dreams have become reality through the tireless dedication of teams of volunteer assistants. Over two years in the making, this tribute to the patroness of Los Angeles shall truly be remembered. We are proud to be able to present this special cultural event and hope that you and your family will partake fully in the magic and genius of Tony Duquette.

Hutton J. Wilkinson
Executive Director,
Anthony & Elizabeth Duquette
Foundation for the
Living Arts

"It is not known precisely where angels dwell, whether in the air, in the void, or the planets. It has not been God's pleasure," wrote Voltaire in his *Philosophical Dictionary*, "that we should be informed of their abode."

In celebration of Los Angeles it has been the pleasure of Artist-Designer Tony Duquette to summon forth from his boundless imagination (and spacious studios) a vast, plumed procession of shining angels. Duquette's heavenly horde of feathered cherubim and seraphim, and his eight golden 24-foot archangels, his huge, glittering, brocaded and jewel-studded tapestries, and—most importantly—the crowned and winged throne of Our Lady, are magical and powerful in their grandeur. For the angelic multitude Duquette has assembled in this hall the Court of the Virgin Mary, Handmaiden of the Lord, Mother of God, Mother of all Nature, Mother of all Mankind, Queen of Heaven and Earth, Queen of the Angels, female superstar of all Eternity, and, somewhat anticlimatically, Patron Saint of this city.

"That minister of ministers,
Imagination, fathers up
The undiscovered universe
Like jewels in a jasper cup."*

Duquette has cloaked Mary, loveliest of all women, in mystery and splendor, and filled the air about her adoring court with strange, sweet music and strange, sweet motion.

Duquette's environment of joyous holiness is certainly not worthy of Heaven's real décor. But in its power to enchant eye and ear, lift up the heart and enthrall the spirit, it far surpasses any *mis en scene* ever designed by Hollywood, even in its most tinseled days of star-studded extravaganzas.

*John Davidson–*There is a Dish to Hold the Sea*
Honolulu, Hawaii

There has not been in the history of art, nor is there today in the art world, a designer of spectacles and environments with more imagination than Duquette. If he had lived in the days of the great monarchs and art-loving princes of Europe, they would have vied furiously with one another to engage his creative services for their balls, fêtes, pageants, processions, stage and opera sets, ceremonials and spectacles.

Do Lorenzo the Magnificent, or Louis XIV, the Sun King, has opened a munificent purse to provide Duquette with the worldly means for his other-worldly Court of Angels. With a few friends, and using his own resources, Duquette has created this gorgeous "celebrational environment" as his gift to the City of Los Angeles. It will be enjoyed by everyone, young or old, whose heart is also on the side of the Angels.

Clare Boothe Luce

The Honorable Clare Boothe Luce

What is a "celebrational environment"? It is not an "exhibit." It is not a "happening." It is something that involves YOU – the people of Los Angeles –

young and old,
poor and rich,
black and white.

When you come, in large or small groups, and stroll around these vast, dim, 10,000 square feet of space, then, and then only, will there be a "celebration" for the City of Our Lady, the Queen of the Angels.

The space is vast. The things it holds are colossal and dreamlike. But they will not make you small. You will *feel* them, as well as *see* them; your consciousness will be expanded by specially-composed poetry and music. And, by a strange illusion, you yourself will become vast and colossal.

This is because religious art and folk art – the two sources of this fantasy "celebration" – do something curious that is called *trompe l'oeil* ("fool the eye"). Have you ever looked at a tiny New Mexico *santo*, carved from cottonwood or gypsum, and riding in a painted "death cart" – and seen it suddenly look as huge as the granite peaks of the Mountains of the Blood of Christ glowing crimson in the sunset? Have you ever noticed that a folk-costume – of Asian *ikat* weaving or American goosequill embroidery – can, all of a sudden, make the wearer seem many times life-sized?

Yes, you will become unaccountably larger, and will be transported – for a time – into another world, another world that is somehow your own.

Although the Madonna who gave her name to Los Angeles is revered in the Catholic church, this "celebrational environment" is for Catholics and non-Catholics, for people of many nationalities, races, and creeds. For the Lady whom you will see has ever-changing faces –

      white,
      yellow,
      red, and
      black –

and she symbolizes universal and eternal figures: Demeter, Cybele, Isis, the Earth Mother, the Mother Earth.

Some 14 feet high, this lady is the central figure of the "environment." She is crowned by a lacy winged dome, guarded by gigantic skeletal angels that tower over her, surrounded by altars and great jewelled tapestries that fill the walls.

o the votive lights – in monumental pyramids of 60 – twinkle from afar? They are measuring the invisible. Are the archangels (the coral, the feathered, the shell archangels) strange and tall? They are capturing infinite space. Overhead, do the enormous gauzy, wing-shaped banners seem to float away in the ceiling? They are defying gravity.

ragile networks of light-rays fill the air, like a procession of invisible dancers who move slowly, gently, beautifully, as in an ancient court masque. Like the spectators, these Beings seem also to be present at the celebration, the festival, the fiesta, the fête.

old is everywhere, gold and more gold – on Virgins, angels, altars, tapestries. But gold for its healing nature, not for conscious decoration. The Incas believed gold to heal; primitive man, lacking gold, attributed this magic power to copper.

oral and mauve, apple green, silver and bronze – these colors and many, many others glimmer from the tapestries. 24 in all . . . created from 8 miles of fabric cut into 826,440 pieces . . . with antique brocades from Macao, Ching Mai,

Thailand, France . . . they show the Angel of Day, the Angel of Night, cherubic and seraphic figures even of Egyptian and Maya inspiration. Our Lady of Africa is here, with her beautiful black face. Four Angels of the Forest, as well as the legions of the Heavenly Host, again have faces in

white,

yellow

red, and

black –

to stress, over and over, the brotherhood of man, which is an implied theme of this "celebration."

Suggested, too, though never stated, is the theme of Nature herself. Shells and feathers have become armor for archangels; the Lady is surrounded with cloth that apotheosizes, that suggests . . . sunset and flowering trees, the iridescence of beetles and birds' wings, the patterns of plumage, scales, and skins, the elegance and great style of insects . . .

Because sight is enriched not only by changing light and waving motion, but also by continual sound, special tapes have been composed and prepared for the "celebrational environment."

Los Angeles' foremost writer, Ray Bradbury, has composed in verse a "saeta" to the Madonna – far longer and more beautiful than those sung in the churches of Seville. Called "A Walk in the

Green Garden of the Queen of the Angels," it is read by the celebrated actor Charlton Heston.

To complete the marriage of "son et lumière" – "sound and light" – Garth Hudson, composer-member of The Band (that same Band that was formerly with Bob Dylan), has created an extraordinary piece of music on a Synthesizer. As much a part of the overall audio concept as Bradbury's sonorous lines, these musical sounds will help to expand the visitor's consciousness – the tapes filling his ears, as the dream-constructions fill his eyes.

It is my hope – and "hope is the thing with feathers that perches on the soul" – that this "celebrational environment," into which I have poured the aspirations of a lifetime, will transport the viewer into another dimension. The dimension beyond.

Tony Marquette

Central to the environment is the Lady Herself: OUR LADY THE QUEEN OF THE ANGELS.

She is 14 feet tall; her face is a shimmering radiance. But not one face alone, *four* faces (constantly changing, electronically) representing the four great ethnic groups of mankind:

    white,
    yellow,
    red, and
    black.

Her crown is of beaded flowers. The symbolic pomegranate and white rose, the lily of virginity and the violet of humility, the iris. Her dress, trimmed with silver lace, adorned with three bouquets of pearls and jewels, is woven to represent the Four Seasons. Over her head, a delicate crown-like halo. All around, holding it up, a lacy openwork pavilion, its 8 sides ornamented with gold wings. And far, far overhead, in the light-motes that seem a part of the environment, gently fluttering banners and enormous, transparent gauzy wings.

The lady is surrounded – and protected – by EIGHT GREAT SKELETAL ARCHANGELS, each one 28 feet tall.

Michael

The greatest of all angels, SAN MIGUEL ARCANGEL, is a transparent, almost-organic figure, who seems to grow from coral. He is generalissimo of the Heavenly Hosts, and will don his armor with the red roses and unsheath his shining sword, when he overcomes the arch-foe, Satan. It was he who destroyed the city of Babylon, and won the battle of Sennacherib – which Byron describes so vividly:

> The Assyrian came down like a wolf on
>   the fold,
> And his cohorts were gleaming with
>   purple and gold,
> And the sheen of their spears was like
>   stars on the sea
> When the blue wave rolls nightly o'er
>   deep Galilee.

Called Mika'il by the Muslims, he is the angel of Righteousness and Mercy; when he weeps, his tears become precious stones. Michael ("who is as God") can hold a pen as well as a sword: he is supposed to have personally written the 85th Psalm. Perhaps he will even put an end to the current wave of violence – for, in 1950, the Vatican declared him the patron of policemen!

Gabriel
Shown as a "seashell" angel, pale and
opalescent with wings of blue silk gauze,
SAN GABRIEL ARCANGEL – whose
flower is the carnation – appeared to the
Virgin to announce the coming birth of
Christ. And it is he who will blow the
"trump of doom" to announce the Last
Judgment. In between these two major
events, Gabriel ("God is my strength") has
watched impartially over mankind in
general. Called Jibril in Arabic, he is
supposed to have dictated the entire Koran
to Mohammed, *sura* by *sura*.

GABRIEL

Raphael

The ARCANGEL SAN RAFAEL rises here out of golden palm-leaves, hung with cut crystals, for it was he who guarded the Tree of Life in the Garden of Eden. Raphael ("God has healed") is the angelic physician. He cured the blind eyes of Tobit with a fish; he healed Jacob of a wound in his thigh; he even handed Noah a "medical book" after the flood! Most sociable of angels, he sat down to supper with Adam and Eve.

Uriel

Made of carved wooden 18th-century plumes, the great angel URIEL is a golden peridot-green in color. He is the angel with the Fiery Sword (his name means "fire of God") who drove Adam and Eve out of Eden; we show him with a flame coming out of the top of his head. A great alchemist, Uriel came down to earth from Heaven in a chariot drawn by white horses.

Israfel

The figure of ISRAFEL, angel of Music, has been cast from 18th-century carvings. His heart-strings are a lute; he invented the lyre, and was the sweetest of singers. Very tall, his feet are under the "seventh earth," and his head reaches the divine throne. Perhaps because of his size, he was one of the archangels sent (in Islamic lore) to the four corners of the earth, to bring back the seven handfuls of dust from which God created Adam.

Ariel
Because he is Lord of the Winds and the
Green Earth, the figure of ARIEL has been
made from malachite, copper, and emeralds.
In this archangel, each spectator can find
whatever he seeks, for he has been called a
city . . . an altar . . . and a man . . . as well as
an angel. Shakespeare turned Ariel into a
sprite; the poet Shelley referred to himself
as Ariel.

Zadkiel

The archangel ZADKIEL has been built of feathers – peacock-feathers, parrot-feathers, whole doves – for he rules over the People of the Birds, Small Birds, Wild Fowl and Creeping Things. Merciful and benevolent, Zadkiel is always ready to prevent trouble. It was he who held back the hand of Abraham when he would have sacrificed his son Isaac.

Azrael

Never cruel, but of a "fearful gentleness" is AZRAEL ("whom God helps") – the angel of Death. This strange and thrilling figure is crowned and adorned with horns and skulls – molded skulls, crocodile skulls – like the Hindu god and goddess Shiva and Kali. His body and wings are covered with dominoes of gold. Azrael writes forever in a large book, and then erases what he has written. He writes the birth of man; he erases the name of the man at death. He separates body from soul by holding an apple from the Tree of Life to the nostril of the dying person. That death is both natural and restful was well understood by Howard Pyle, who presents the angel of Death as a wonderful being in his children's classic, *The Garden behind the Moon*.

AZRAEL

**On the lofty walls of the "celebration,"
EIGHT LARGE TAPESTRIES, nearly
20 feet by 20 feet, shimmer and appear
to move in the dimness.**

Angel of Day

On a light blue sky, with silver rays radiating from his head and body (as from the sun's wheel) is the ANGEL OF DAY. He is a Being of Light, an emissary of the Solar Logos. Called SHAMSHIEL ("mighty sun of God"), he wears a cloak of shining "chasmal," and has a radiant halo. A crown of gold is his thought; it is set with many jewels, each one an idea. In Sanskrit, he is described as Chitra Shikandina – a bright-crested one. In ancient Persia, he was Chur, angel of the Disc of the Sun.

Angel of Night

The ANGEL OF NIGHT is not a force of evil, but the counterpart of the Angel of Day. He is called LAILAHEL, and sheds a golden radiance over a dark blue midnight sky. His attendants, two kneeling figures, are Angels of the Mansions of the Moon. In the border of the tapestry, we can make out his 36 pairs of wings and his 365,000 eyes for seeing in the dark!

Our Lady of Africa

Here, with her beautiful black face and an irridescent overlay of silk gauzes, is OUR LADY OF AFRICA. She reaches out even beyond Christianity – for Muslim women call her LALA MERIEM and ask for her *haraka* (or blessing) to send good husbands, to cure illness, to stop famines.

Famous black-faced Madonnas are also found in Spain, like La Moreneta ("The Little Dark One") of Montserrat. But most famous of all is the black Virgin of Czestochowa – patroness of Poland, homeland of the present Pope.

Supposedly painted by St. Luke on a table made by Jesus as an apprentice carpenter, and found by the mother of the Emperor Constantine, the black MADONNA OF CZESTOCHOWA was hidden in the forests of Belsk in Eastern Poland, and finally taken to Czestochowa by a Prince instructed by an angel in a dream. She is credited with the survival of the Polish nation against all invaders to the present day. Protected from murderous and looting Tartars by a cloud,

and from thieving and burning Hussites by stubborn horses (who would not carry her away, no matter how hard they were beaten), she was cleansed of mud and blood by a miraculous fountain that has healed thousands of sick pilgrims over the centuries. Enshrined today in every church in Poland, she appeared in the clouds above Vistula as late as 1920, and was given public devotion by a crowd of a million and a half Polish citizens only thirty-five years ago.

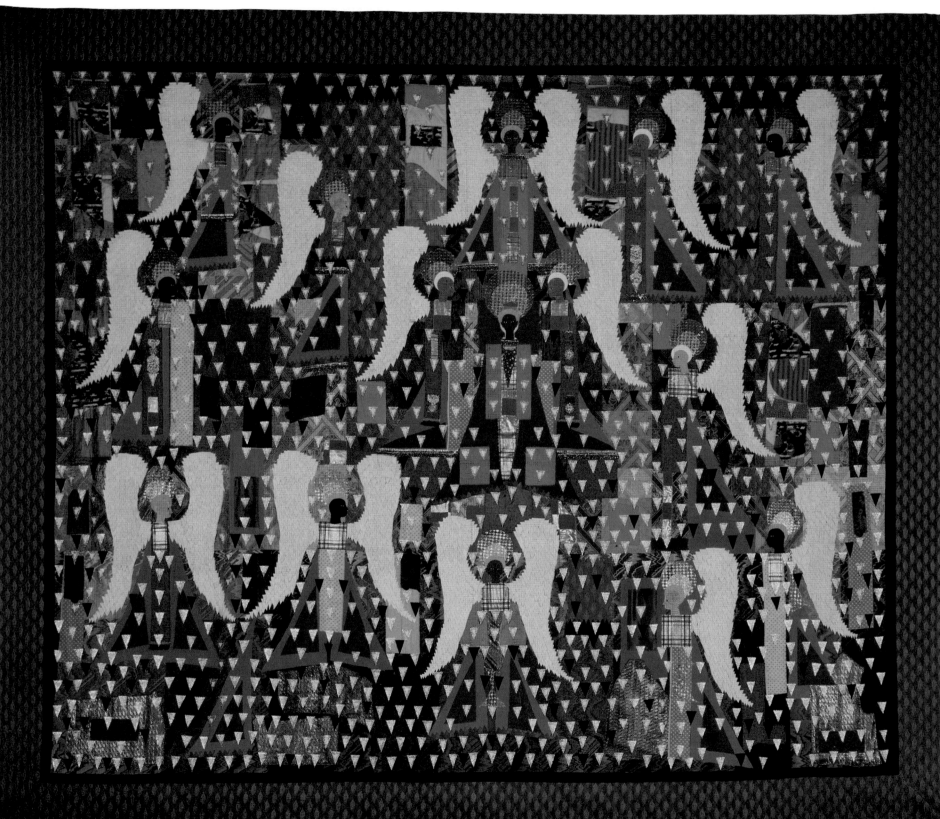

Heavenly Host

Job conceived the HEAVENLY HOST as morning stars singing together and shouting for joy. But this "celebration" conceives them as the four great ethnic divisons of mankind – with faces

white,
yellow,
red, and
black.

They are Enoch's Angel Princes – Archangels, Angels, Principalities, Virtues, Dominions, Powers, Thrones, Cherubim, and Seraphim – and correspond to the Devas of Eastern religions. Cherubs have been shown as playful children, or Beings with four faces (Man, Eagle, Lion, Ox); here they take a manlike form in sign of universal brotherhood.

Egyptian Angel
On a ground of burlap, appliquéd with
metallic cloth and overlaid with saffron
gauze, we have an EGYPTIAN ANGEL. He
is not one of the evil angels who fought
against the Israelites, but the good TEHUTI.
Like the Christian Recording angel, like the
Lipika of Hinduism, he writes in a great
book the deeds of all men, by which they
shall be judged. Tehuti is a lawgiver and
chronologer.

Mexican Angel
7,000 tassels are woven into this brilliant copper, green, and golden tapestry of the Mexican angel KAKUPACAT, Señor of the Volcanoes. He is one of the four Mayan archangels, or Bacabes, who guard the Four Quarters of the earth: the North, which is white; the South, which is yellow; the East, which is red; and the West, which is black.

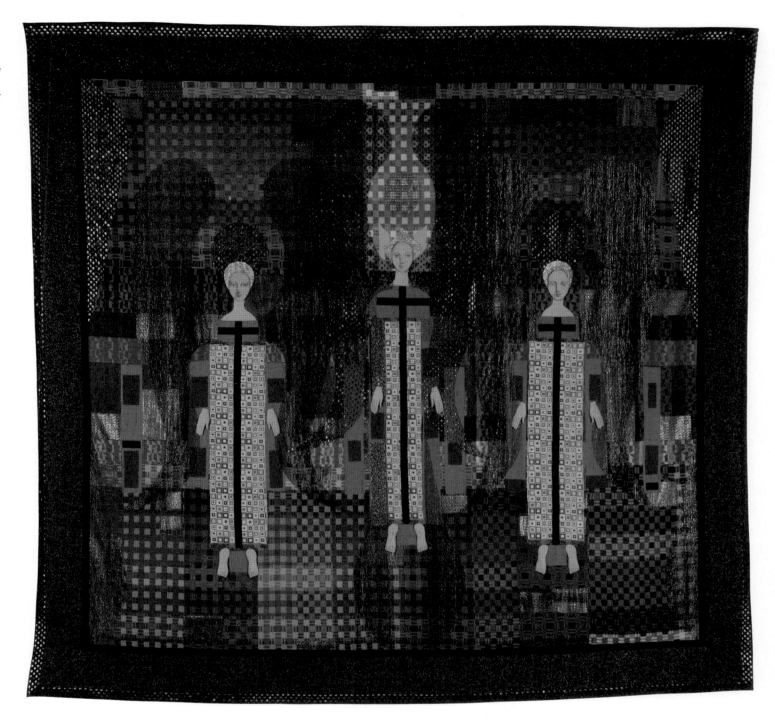

Three Aquarian Angels
Included for the younger generation of the coming "Age of Aquarius" are its three rulers: the angels AUSIUL, ARCHER, and SSAKMAKIEL. They have dominion over Aquarius, over water, even over water insects; they are invoked by magical rites.

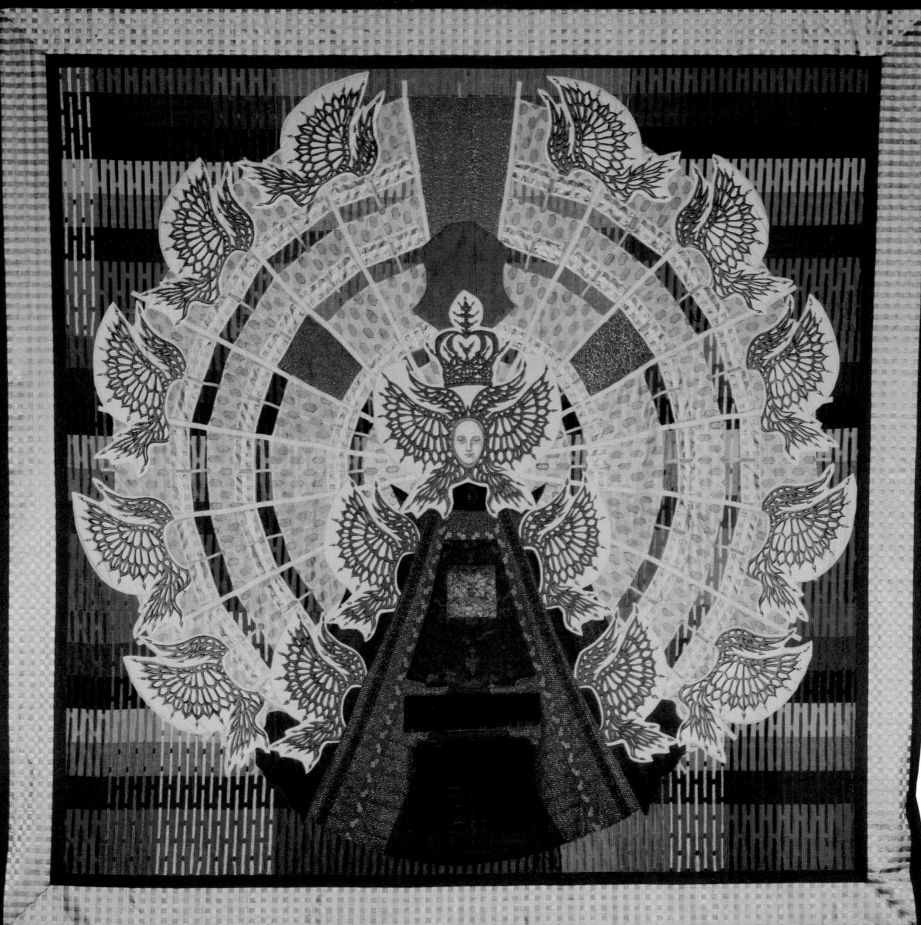

The Radiance
Like the central figure of our celebration,
this tapestry pictures the Lady herself:
NUESTRA SEÑORA LA REINA DE LOS
ANGELES DE PORCIÚNCULA – Our
Lady the Queen of the Angels, whose town
is on the River Porciúncula. She has a
wingéd halo, a wingéd robe, a golden crown.
Behind her – like an open fan – is an
interlacing of woven tassels and shaded
stripes in gold, beige, gray, burnt orange, teal
blue. Suggested, rather than shown, are her
symbols: bees and apples, "lady's slippers,"
and ears of corn.

As he strolls around the "environment," the visitor will see SIXTEEN SMALLER TAPESTRIES, most of them 8 feet by 12 feet.

Asian Angel
The serene white face is that of the Asian ANGEL OF THE PURE LAND OF THE WEST. She is one of the seven-thousand-times-seven-thousand Celestial maidens or APSARAS – corresponding very closely to the "myriads" (or ten-thousand-times-ten-thousand) of the Angelic Hosts. Around her, we glimpse the gold, silver, beryl, crystal, coral, red pearls, and emerald vegetation of a Paradise that strikingly resembles St. Augustine's "City of God."

San Miguel Arcangel
In this tapestry, the archangel MICHAEL –
one of the Celestial Triumvirate of the three
most cherished archangels – appears once
more. Here, he wears a starred coat of gold
and gunmetal armor. Like the great warrior
he is, he carries two flaming swords of
yellow and orange.

Angel of the Knights of Malta
Chivalric tradition and Egyptian Freemasonry mingle to produce the legendary ANGEL OF THE KNIGHTS OF MALTA. His dark hands and face suggest yet another source, a Moorish one. Note his magnificent silver and scarlet jewelled "heaume" or casque; his silver and blue armor; and, strangest of all, the Eye of Horus that appears both on his bosom and over his head.

Sainted Angel

A story tells that St. Anne, the Mother of
the Virgin, ascended to Heaven – where she
was transformed into the angel ANAS. Here,
her compassionate face is surrounded by a
lavender and scarlet aureola. Her gentle
hands are outspread from her silvery mantle
and pale, pale dress.*

*This tapestry is gratefully dedicated to the Annes
and the many volunteers who worked on the
"celebrational environment."

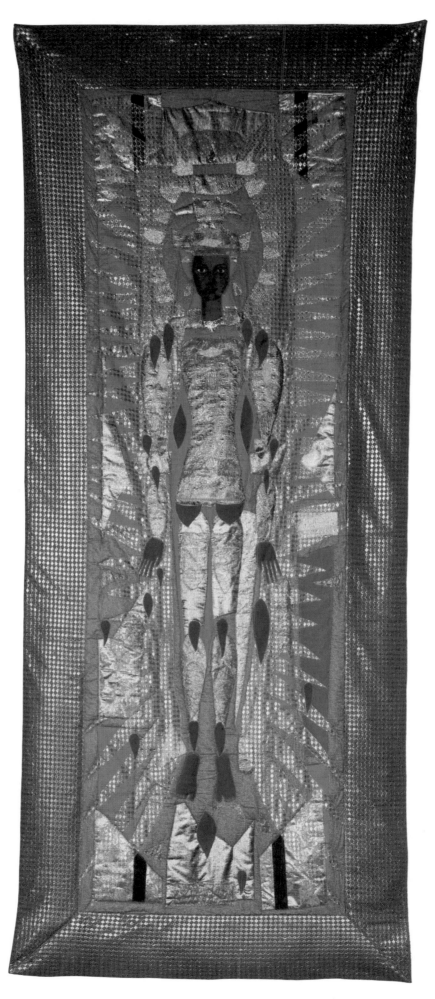

Angel of the Flame

The angel NATHANIEL, sometimes wrongly called "El Auria," is shown on a background of old rose, with blue flames radiating in every direction from his entire body. He parallels the Zoroastrian incarnation of fire, Atar, and the Vedic one, Agni. When the wicked idolater Jair ordered seven men faithful to God to be thrown into a bonfire, Nathanial ("Lord over fire") put out the flames and helped the men escape. The modern Russian composer Prokofieff has written an opera called "L'Ange de Feu" – "The Angel of Fire" – which was premiered in New York fifteen years ago. The chief character is the Angel MADIEL, who appears to the heroine (a 16th-century lady) in the form of a German knight.

Gemini Angels

Which twins are these . . . ? They could be METATRON and SANDALPHON, tallest of all the Heavenly Princes – one of whom showed himself as a pillar of fire, while the other parted the Red Sea and led the Children of Israel through the wildnerness . .

Or they could be the IRIN OR QADDISIN, two pairs of high-ranking angel "watchers" who make up the supreme judgment council of Heaven's court . . . Yet again, they could be the HOCUS and POCUS of incantation, whose names are derived from the Latin sentence *"Hoc est corpus meum"* – "This is my body" . . . It is for the viewer to interpret these golden wings, this patchwork of orange and orchid.

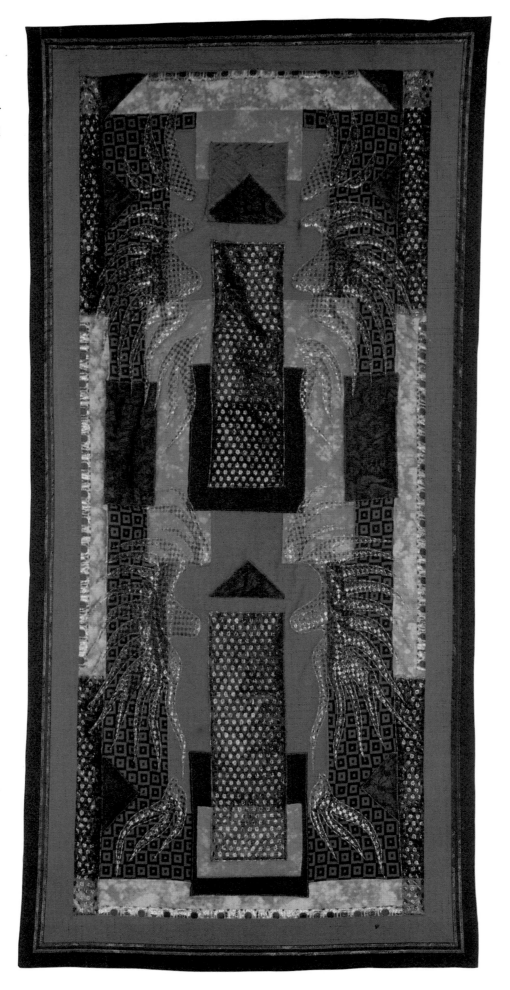

Malachite Seraphs of the North, South, East, and West

These four SERAPHIM repeat the brotherly theme of our "environment," for their faces portray the four ethnic groups of humanity:

> white,
> yellow,
> red, and
> black.

They control the four winds and uphold the earth. Around the throne of God, they endlessly chant the "trisagion": "Holy, holy, holy!" The contemporary artist Marc Chagall is not the first to paint them; they were pictured in the 15th century, playing on the viola d'amore. Malachite and other precious stones are sacred to them.

**First and Second Angels of the
Wild Beasts**
These two tapestries portray MTNIEL and
JEHIEL, two Cherubim with dominion
over wild beasts. Jungle spirits of southeast
Asia seem to appear in the gold-spotted
brown that suggests fur. And they are kin
to other southeast Asian Beings: the Garuda
birds, which have the faces of men and the
wings of angels.

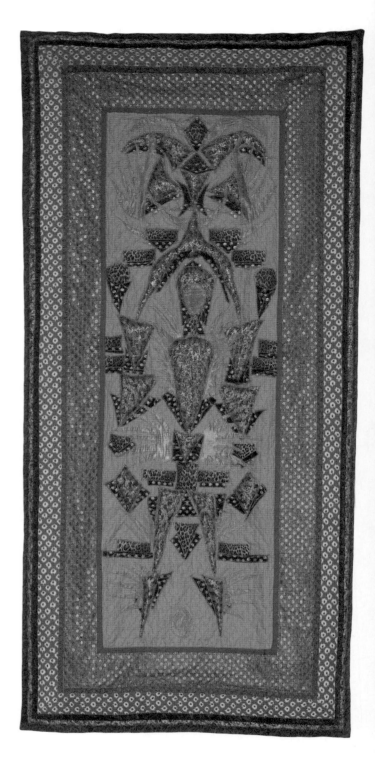

Two Aspects of the Angel of the Forest
Companion-pieces, these tapestries show
two aspects of ZUPHLAS, angel of the
Forest. In one, he is symbolized by a green
obelisk – the green of trees. In the other, by
a primrose-colored obelisk: "rosy-tipped
dawn" (Homer's phrase) is filtering into
a forest clearing. The wings, as usual, are
golden; the forest itself is in many shades
of green.

The four "elements" of antiquity –
Earth, Air, Fire, Water – are symbolized
by FOUR ALTARS TO OUR LADY, set
against the walls of the "celebrational
environment."

Of Spanish, Italian, and Mexican origin, all
four of these Madonnas – and often their
gowns, cloaks, and crowns (even their
chapels or shrines) are assemblages from the
17th, 18th, and early 19th centuries. But the
fantasy-vision of the 20th century brings
them to life for our day.

Altar of Earth*
A neo-Gothic reredos grows out of gnarled
grape-roots. The Virgin wears a crown of
wheat and pearls.

Dedicated to Elsie de Wolfe, Lady Mendl

Altar of Air**
Three pavilions are upheld by birds—these represent the angels of the Air: Chasan, Casmaron, Cherub, and Iahmel. The Virgin wears a Thai cloak made from thousands of feathers.

**Dedicated to Mary Palmer Gross

Altar of Fire***
A giant golden sunburst from an Austrian church hangs over an antique Spanish altar case holding an 18th century Portuguese Madonna. The candlesticks are Venetian.

***Dedicated to Bessie Führer Erb, Elsa Führer Duquette, and Lucy Führer Genter

Altar of Water**
The undersea altar is inspired by the old
French legend of "the engulfed cathedral." It
is the altar of that cathedral encrusted with
sea shells and barnacles over the centuries.
The antique bead flower bouquets have
sea shells, coral, and pearls added and the
antique Madonna in the 18th century Italian
shrine wears a crown of coral and pearls.
The tapestry in the center is an abstract
representation of the Angel of Aspirations
and Dreams.

*****Dedicated to Alice Larkin Tuolmin*

Ray Bradbury

**A Walk in the Green Garden
of the Queen of the Angels
A *Celebration*
By Ray Bradbury**

Ithuriel . . . Ithoth . . . Itqal . . . Israfel . . . Iofiel . . . Iaeo!
    Ithuriel! Ithoth! Itqal . . .
Know all . . . cover all . . . shield all . . . protect all . . .
    with your love!
Above the forest of women . . . shadow and move . . .
    hover and fly!

Elemiah! Elilaios!
Fine Ephemerae, come this way!
Make a roof above this forest,
Where the many Maidens stay.
Where the Mother of the Angels
With her bright Sun Flesh abides,
Where Madonna moonfires gather
In processionals of brides . . .
Brides . . . brides . . . brides . . .

Here the Earth grows up as Mother . . .
Sweet Demeter, Cybele mild.
Here the Harvest comes as Mary . . .
And *her* Harvest: Divine Child.

Mithra . . . Mitatron . . . Mibi . . .
Michael . . . Burning Bright!
Memsiel and Mendrion . . .
Guard the Virgin's sleep by night.
Seven angels, greater still,
Rise in thunders on the sill!
Gabriel! Zadkiel! Hadriel! Uriel! Michael, now . . .
     and San Rafael . . .
Then Ariel, who sings . . .
Stand above the Queen of Angels,
And protect her with your wings!

O the many Mothers of all time . . .
The many faces and the many hands
From all the lands of living
What magnificence of giving.
Many whisperings of graces,
Multitudes of gentle faces,
Many colors, many names
From many places.

Skin like amber,
Skin like silk.
Skin like umber
Skin like milk.
White as snow upon the mountain,
Clear as freshet-water fountain;
Dark as coffee, shadowed night,
Then as quickly, burning bright.
Madre mia, mothers few,
Mothers many rise to view.

Madre mia, Madrecita, holy Mother, Virgin bright,
Gather by the tens of thousands,
With your constellation light
Every corner, every cradle,
Every sleeping room at night
With your heart and blood and dreaming
With your first and second sight.
Many mothers for our children,
Many faces, many hands,
Come to us from many lands.

Multitudinous your loving,
Multitudinous in holy sound
Now on all sides manifested
Come and every soul surround.
Everywhere we turn we find you
In the candle-burning night
Blessed Virgin, Madre mia, Madrecita
Burning bright.

Brothers, sisters, sisters, brothers
Gather here and grow us tall.
Where a thousand thousand Mothers
Holy make this gathering hall.
Voices sing us, shadows ring us
Here and here and here again,
Mothers,
          mothers,
                    send your blessings
Like a gentle, falling rain.

Multitudinous and many
Like a forest ring us 'round,
Like a field of wheat and flowers
Queen of Angels' holy ground.

Queen of Angels . . . Queen of Angels
Hear the naming, see her face . . .
Put her name upon this city,
Make Los Angeles her place . . .
Make Los Angeles her place!

Queen of Angels . . . Queen of Angels!

Ithuriel . . . Ithoth . . . Itqual! Israfel! Iofiel!
Know all . . . cover all . . . shield all . . . protect all . . .
        with your love.
Fine Ephemerae, now Michael, San Rafael, come this way.
Make a roof above this forest
Where the Queen of Angels stays.

Hear her naming, see her face.
Put her name upon this city.
Make Los Angeles her place.
Make Los Angeles her place!

Catalog Designed by
Nourse Graham Costain & Associates

Photography by
James Chen